Cinnamon Grits

Christmas in the South

Written by
Erica McGee

Original Score by
Erica McGee

STEELE SPRING
STAGE RIGHTS
www.stagerights.com

CINNAMON GRITS: CHRISTMAS IN THE SOUTH

For all stage performance inquiries, please contact:

STEELE SPRING STAGE RIGHTS

Steele Spring Stage Rights
3845 Cazador Street
Los Angeles, CA 90065 (323) 739-0413
www.stagerights.com

Cinnamon GRITS

Christmas in the South

PRODUCTION HISTORY

The world premiere production of *Cinnamon GRITS: Christmas in the South* opened at Niswonger Performing Arts Center in Greeneville, TN on December 2010.

Written by Erica Allen McGee
Directed by Erica Allen McGee
Choreography: Bryan J. Wlas
Musical Direction: Erica Allen McGee
Score Arrangements: Michael Van Patter
Set Design: Erica Allen McGee
Costume Design: Erica Allen McGee
Lighting Design: Hallie Gray
Props Design: Erica Allen McGee/Ashley Hawkins
Production Stage Manager: Ashley Hawkins

Cast:

Virginia.. Ginger Newman
Georgia ....Erica Allen McGee
Flo ....Asia Craft
Charlotte...Elizabeth Lucin

CHARACTER DESCRIPTIONS

(1) **CHARLOTTE:** 20-ish college grad, bubbly and fun, soprano.

(2) **GEORGIA:** 30-ish society gal, put-together mom, alto.

(3) **VIRGINIA:** 50-60-ish sassy, mature-type, can do it all, soprano.

(4) **FLORENCE "FLO":** 30-40-ish African American mom with attitude, alto.

STAGING DIRECTIONS

The set is like a cozy living room. Two Christmas trees are on the stage with toys beneath and wrapped gifts, one SL and one SR. Gifts are under the tree. A fireplace is center stage. There are parsons-style bar stools decorated with chair covers that are holiday colors or rocking chairs. They split the fireplace DS. The screen behind them depicts a window that changes images with each story and song performed.

The basic direction of the show is as follows. The opening monologue is an introduction to the flow of the production. It is to have an explanatory feel. The opening music number is to introduce the "characters" to the audience. Each actor is more of a "personality" than a "character" as they will change from scene to scene with the telling of the individual stories. Casting is crucial in that the actors need to have their own uniqueness to flow from scene to scene while still being able to portray the character in each monologue.

A quote from a famous "GRITS Girl" will introduce each scene. The quotes are delivered from one actor and another actor will then deliver the scene.

CINNAMON GRITS
Christmas in the South

AUTHOR'S NOTE

Honestly, *Cinnamon GRITS: Christmas in the South* started out as a project based on requests. I had almost every theater that had done *Girls Raised in the South-GRITS: The Musical* ask me when I was going to do a Christmas version of the show. So, I did. BUT, what happened when I started to write and collect stories and interview friends and family was something that I never expected. These stories were ALL personal to ME. This show is not based on an already existing work, and so, what I found was my own voice. I found out what was important for me to share. The holidays can be wonderful and awful. Fulfilling and desperate. It's a season filled with lots of different things to a lot of different people, so, what I wove together in this project were the things that made me FEEL. Stories that resonated with multiple friends, family, and colleges. Humor and sentiment, insanity and stability, all of which are thrust at us during that time of year. And don't we love it all. The music in this show was truly personal to me and I hope that the audience can hear that. Family gatherings and the celebration of who we are and what we love is what this piece is all about! I hope that it is a show that truly represents so many things that we hold dear during that most wonderful time of the year!

CINNAMON GRITS

Christmas in the South

MUSICAL NUMBERS

ACT I

Scene 1

1. Christmas in the South (Waltz) .... Company

Scene 2

2. Jingle All the Way (Polka)................................Company, featuring Woman 3

Scene 3

3. The Perfect Gift (Ballad/Pop)... Woman 2

Scene 4

4. Do the Regift! (Upbeat R&B)... Woman 4

Scene 5

5. I Never Knew Life Without You (Ballad/Pop) .... Woman 1

Scene 6

6. The Crazy Aunt Blues (Upbeat/Blues) ....Company, featuring Woman 2

Scene 7

7. The Twelve Yummy Days of Christmas (Upbeat/Traditional).........Company

MUSICAL NUMBERS (CONT'D)

ACT II

Scene 1

8. Belle Medley (Upbeat/Traditional) .... Company
    - Caroling, Caroling
    - Carol of the Bells
    - Silver Bells

Scene 2

9. Yes, There Is a Santa Claus (Doo-Wop) .... Woman 1

Scene 3

10. Carolina Christmas (Country) .... Woman 2

Scene 4

11. What the River May Hold (Cajun Blues) .... Woman 4

Scene 5

12. I Want to See You/Away in a Manger *(*Ballad/Carol Traditional) ....
....Woman 3 & Woman 1

Scene 6

13. Christmas Carol Medley .... Company
    - Silent Night
    - Oh Holy Night
    - Joyful, Joyful We Adore Thee
    - Joy to the World

ACT I

WOMAN 2 enters carrying a present.

WOMAN 2: Oh hey! Merry Christmas y'all! You know, the holidays are very important to us GRITS. That's Girls Raised in the South y'all! In fact, did you know the first three states in America to recognize Christmas as a legal holiday were Southern ones? Louisiana, Arkansas and Alabama made it official in the mid-1800s. Southerners regard Christmas as both a holy day and a holiday. All kinds of traditions from all over the world grace our landscape. While much of the rest of the world will spend the holiday season nestled under a snowy blanket, for most of the South that just isn't so. In some parts of the South we've even been known, on occasion, to see a White Christmas. Flakes glistening on window sills, fields and gardens covered up like white fluffy clouds. But, in many parts of the South, December snow would be a phenomenon... something to put in the memory books. For us, Christmas is about greenery and blooming flowers, mild afternoons and evenings with the heat on low, maybe a log in the fireplace for ambiance. And even though Christmas in the South means we may hear the red bird sing, it IS still Christmas and Christmas is beyond climate... beyond geography... because Christmas is found at home.

SONG #1: CHRISTMAS IN THE SOUTH

WOMAN 1:
SNOWY COVERED PINECONES

WOMAN 4:
FIRE ON LOW

WOMAN 3:
IT'S THAT TIME OF YEAR WHEN HOPE AND CHEER WILL REAPPEAR

WOMAN 2:
LIGHTS UPON A TREE WITH THE ONES YOU LOVE
POUR ANOTHER GLASS OF EGGNOG

ALL:
CHRISTMAS IN THE SOUTH, THAT'S WHAT WE'RE ALL ABOUT

WOMAN 1:
SO, WE WISH FOR YOU

WOMAN 4:
CHRISTMAS DREAMS COME TRUE

WOMAN 2:
AND GOOD MEMORIES MADE NEW

WOMAN 1, 4:
THE POINSETTIAS IN BLOOM

WOMAN 2, 3:
AND FAMILY'S COMING HOME SOON

WOMAN 4:
SNOWY COVERED PINECONES

WOMAN 3:
FIRE ON LOW

WOMAN 2:
IT'S THAT TIME OF YEAR WHEN HOPE AND CHEER WILL REAPPEAR

WOMAN 1:
SO WE WISH FOR YOU

WOMAN 3:
CHRISTMAS DREAMS COME TRUE

ALL:
AND GOOD MEMORIES MADE NEW!

WOMAN 4: "Santa baby, slip a sable under the tree, for me. I've been an awful good girl. Santa baby, and hurry down the chimney tonight" –A quote from Eartha Kitt, GRITS Gal from South Carolina

WOMAN 3: My son-in-law is a writer from North Carolina. He says that a person's most important tool in life is the power of observation. Well...let's just say that's never been one of my gifts. I suppose as I have gotten older that the power of distraction has become one of my more predominant traits and as the stress level rises, the attention to detail has been known to suffer. So, it should come as no surprise that during the holiday season, with all the gift lists, sales, coupons, holiday cards, and general Christmas mayhem that I would, from time to time, have a lapse in awareness.

I was at my favorite discount department store, you know the ones... they have everything and nothing all in the same store. I had been toying with the idea of getting that season's HOT Christmas gift, THE SNUGGIE [*OR whatever the HOT Christmas item is for that season]*, for my daughter! I pushed my buggy over to the 12-foot pyramid of these "must have" items and went to check out, leopard print SNUGGIE in hand.

I gave my items to the cashier, wished her a "Merry Christmas" with the utmost holiday cheer and rolled towards the exit.

As I looked down into my buggy, I couldn't believe my eyes! Someone had stolen my shopping bags with all of my gifts right out of my cart! I quickly retraced my steps...nothing. I decided I had to tell someone so I went to the customer service desk, and the store manager was in shock! She responded with "OH NO THEY DID NOT!" and grabbed the intercom microphone. She was going into full scale, code red, lock down! I was so excited that I clapped my hands together in jubilation. Unfortunately, that joy quickly disappeared as I looked down to see my bags swinging freely from my arms. *(Holds arms out)* They were like really big ugly ornaments *(Swings arms back and forth)* hanging from a poorly decorated Christmas tree. She saw the evidence on my arm, the accuser and the criminal all in one. I simply looked at her and said, "I need to go home."

WOMAN 3 (CONT'D): Shopping and the holidays... not a good combination for me, but the SNUGGIE was a huge hit with my daughter. Hopefully she'll never know I almost sent myself to jail tryin' to buy it!

SONG #2: JINGLE ALL THE WAY

WOMEN enter each chorus carrying lots of shopping bags. As they pass WOMAN 3, they each place one of their bags onto her arms. By the end of the number she is covered in them! She gets more and more tired as the song progresses.

(Singing)

JINGLE BELLS, JINGLE BELLS, JINGLE ALL THE WAY
OH, WHAT FUN IT IS TO GO SHOPPING EVERY DAY
OUTLET MALL, FINE BOUTIUE, WAL-MART AFTER THAT
TOYS FOR ALL THE KIDDIES AND DON'T FORGET AUNT PAT
DASHING THROUGH THE MOBS
RUSHING EVERYWHERE
SQUEEZING THROUGH THE AISLES
TRYING NOT TO SWEAR
FIND THE PERFECT GIFT
OH IT'S NOT ON SALE
CHEAPER ON THE WEBSITE GET FREE SHIPPING IN THE MAIL! YEAH!

ALL:

JINGLE BELLS, JINGLE BELLS HOW THEY LOVE TO RING
I'VE BEEN SHOPPING ALL WEEK LONG AND HAVEN'T FOUND A THING
RINGING LOUD HOW THEY SOUND
THEY WON'T STOP I FEAR

WOMAN 3:

GOOD FOR US THAT CHRISTMAS ONLY COMES BUT ONCE A YEAR!
PLAN YOUR CHRISTMAS MEAL
TWENTY-FOUR TO COME
TURKEY AND A ROAST
WHEN THE COOKIN'S DONE
COUSIN BILL ARIVES
WITH SOME EXTRA FRIENDS
BUT HE DID NOT TELL YOU THAT THEY'RE
VEG-IT-TAR-IANS!

ALL:

OH! JINGLE BELLS, JINGLE BELLS, JINGLE SANTA CLAUS
EIGHTY CHRISTMAS CARDS TO MAIL ARE STITTING IN MY DRAWER!
JINGLE BELLS, JINGLE BELLS, MAIL FROM AUNT PATRICE

WOMAN 3:
OH MY GOSH HER CHRITSMAS LETTER'S LONG AS "WAR AND PEACE"!
JINGLE BELLS, JINGLE BELLS, WHAT A PIERCING TONE
BOUGHT SO MANY GIFTS I'LL HAVE TO TAKE OUT A HOME LOAN.
JINGLE BELLS, JINGLE BELLS, A FEW MORE THINGS TO GET,
(Ritard)
BUT WHEN I SEE THE CHILDREN SMILE
I'LL KNOW IT WAS WORTH IT!

WOMAN 1, 2, 4:
JINGLE BELLS, JINGLE BELLS, JINGLE BELLS! HEY!

WOMAN 1: "Christmas, my child, is love in action. Every time we love, every time we give, it's Christmas." –A quote from Ms. Dale Evans Rodgers– Texas GRITS, American performer and icon.

WOMAN 2: I remember my perfect Christmas gift. You know... the one you cut out of the sale paper and glued to your parents bathroom mirror? Or the one you picked out of the JCPenney catalog in October when your Mom got it in the mail? Mine was the Barbie Dream House, followed by the Barbie Corvette, followed by the Barbie Dream Pool, followed by the... well, you get the picture.

So, I guess it should not have come as any surprise that my daughter became a doll lover. This Christmas I had to send out a warning to all grandparents, aunts, uncles, cousins, second cousins, friends, neighbors and anyone who might even THINK about buying my daughter a gift. We were not, under any circumstances to receive ANY BARBIE dolls. We were, at that time, totaling 57 Barbies in the house, so I declared this to be a BARBIE-free holiday.

Enter Rebecca Rubin. Ever heard of her? *(Acknowledge audience response)* SHE is an AMERICAN GIRL DOLL. Oh yes...that's right, the biggest, baddest, doll of them all, the Cadillac of girl's gifts. Did I mention they are not cheap? You can get a dozen Barbies for one American Girl doll! The minute I declared it a Barbie-free holiday, this was all she could talk about.

Rebecca Rubin. She was the one that my daughter HAD to have. I was drawn to her too. She was beautiful. She had the best clothes, the prettiest accessories, she lived in New York City, AND *(Pause)* she was a Jewish American doll. This was an interesting choice for the little girl who attends Sunday school at Savannah's biggest Baptist Church!

Each type of doll has its own history. She asked me what Rebecca's background was. "Rebecca, the Jewish American doll," I began. "Mom, what's Jewish?" So, I stared with Chanukah and went from there. She was intrigued. And thus, it began.

"How many presents do they get?", "Why do the Shermans next door have a big blue star on their house?", "Do they get to see Santa?" and on and on and on.

WOMAN 2 (CONT'D): I did the best I could, but to be honest, some of the questions were over my head! I found myself Googling Chanukah factoids in the middle of the night. And what did she tell every Santa Claus she saw? "I want an American Girl doll for Christmas. Rebecca Rubin. She's Jewish!"

Christmas morning arrived and sure enough, Santa brought Rebecca Rubin. There she was with her fancy shoes, fabulous bag and all. My daughter was thrilled. Sunday morning came and we all piled in the car and headed off to church, ALL of us, me, my husband, my daughter and Rebecca. As I dropped my daughter off in Sunday school class, I laughed as she entered the room. Her teacher said, "Oh did you get that doll for Christmas?" "Yes! Her name is Rebecca Rubin and she's Jewish!" Her teacher smiled with a slightly confused look on her face as she shut the door, too cute.

That was the year I realized that Christmas is not about what the gift is, it's about the excitement in their eyes. We give to our kids. Attention, praise, and yes sometimes presents, so we can get our gift, that look, that smile. And aren't we lucky? Really look in your child's eyes and it can be the holidays three hundred sixty-five days a year.

SONG #3: THE PERFECT GIFT

(Singing)

CURL UP IN MY LAP AND LET ME SING YOU A SONG
YOU'LL BE GROWN UP BEFORE TOO LONG
EVERYTHING YOU WANT I WANNA GET FOR YOU
I HANG ON EVERYTHING YOU SAY OR DO
AS IT TURNS OUT YOU WERE WHAT I WANTED
NEEDED BUT NEVER KNEW
MY PRESENT WASN'T IN A BOX
MY PERFECT GIFT WAS YOU

TIME IT FLIES AND IT GOES SO FAST
I WANT IT ALL, ALL TO LAST
YOU ARE MY PRINCESS AND MY PRECIOUS DEAR
YOUR VOICE A CAROL TO MY EARS
I HOPE YOU DREAM YOUR GREAT BIG DREAMS
AND THAT THEY ALL COME TRUE
JUST KNOW THAT MINE ALREADY DID
MY PERFECT IN YOU

PRESENTS WRAPPED BENEATH THE TREE
AREN'T WHAT'S IMPORTANT TO ME
PRETTY BOWS AND FANCY THINGS

WOMAN 2 (CONT'D):

MAY BE SIGNS OF GLAD TIDINGS
BUT YOU CAN'T WRAP WHAT I WANNA GET
CAUSE YOU MY DEAR ARE THE PERFECT GIFT

PUT YOUR HEAD ON MY CHEST AND LET ME HOLD YOU TIGHT
IT'S A MAMA'S JOB TO MAKE IT ALRIGHT
I'LL BE THERE WHENEVER YOU CALL MY NAME
I'LL MISS YOU WHEN YOU GO AWAY
DON'T WORRY IF IT GETS TOO HARD
AND YOU DON'T KNOW WHAT TO DO
JUST KNOW THAT YOU'RE ALWAYS LOVED
MY PERFECT GIFT MY YOU
JUST KNOW THAT YOU'RE ALWAYS LOVED
MY PERFECT GIFT MY YOU

WOMAN 3: "It is a dangerous thing to ask why someone else has been given more. It is humbling and indeed healthy to ask why you've been given so much." –A quote from Miss Condaleeza Rice, Former National Security Advisor and Alabama GRITS!

WOMAN 4: Now since it is Christmas time and thus the season of forgiveness, I must confess, I have a dirty little secret. Now before any of you get all worked up, you better know that you all probably have one too. I am a closet re-gifter. *(Gasp!)* I know. Not only am I a closet re-gifter, but I actually have a closet for my gifts to "Re"! Don't judge me. Re-gifting is a longstanding Southern tradition. I mean, waste not want not, right? Most of you probably have a shelf or a drawer at home that houses some things that are nice, they just aren't for you. SO, rather than throw them away, you save 'em for a rainy day when you realize you need just the right thing for that person you totally forgot about.

My re-gifting is an inherited trait. My mom keeps a cabinet above the washer and dryer filled with goodies to give, and my grandmother? One year she gave my mom this really interesting sweater on Christmas day. After dinner we pulled the video out of last year's festivities and as we watched everyone open the gifts from the year before. What did we see? My grandmother receive the exact same sweater that she had just given my Mom. Coincidence? No. Certifiable? Yes. So, see? There was no way I was gonna avoid my re-gifting dysfunction.

You would think I would learn my lesson since I have had a re-gift or two backfire on me. Once I sent my cousin, who lives in Tennessee, a wedding present from my stash. It was a clock that was given to me on my birthday from my crazy Aunt Nadine. It was... unique. I truly thought she would love it. Weeks later I received a thank you note for my thoughtful gift.

WOMAN 4 (CONT'D): "Dear Flo, Thank you so much for the wonderful clock. I was a little confused when I opened it up and there was a card inside that said, "Happy Birthday Flo. Love, the Aunt Nadine."

Busted. But even after all that, my affliction remains. I mean, I promise I'll quit someday. First, I just have to get rid of the whistle key finder, light up shower mirror, cupcake scented bath gels and the leopard print long johns. Any takers?

SONG #4: DO THE RE-GIFT!

Slides in this song need to be taken onstage by WOMAN 4. She wears or holds the items she sings about with a disgusted look on her face. (I.e. she has the cat sweater on and holds up the yard gnome, or the George Foreman grill, etc.) There are marker slides of the original actress in the presentation provided to offer ideas for your individual actresses. This is an important part of this song as it adds a lot of humor and visual effect.

(Singing)

HERE'S MY STORY
YOU MAY RELATE
GETTING A GIFT
IT AIN'T ALWAYS GREAT
ESPECIALLY IF ITS SOMETHING YOU HATE
TAKE MY ADVICE
AND DON'T HESITATE

WOMAN 1, 2, 3:
AND DO THE REGIFT!

WOMAN 4:
A THING YOU DON'T WANT TO OWN

WOMAN 1, 2, 3:
DO THE REGIFT

WOMAN 4:
FIND IT A BRAND-NEW HOME

WOMAN 1, 2, 3:
DO THE REGIFT

WOMAN 4:
YOU'RE NOT BEING MEAN

WOMAN 1, 2, 3:
DO THE REGIFT
IT'S GOOD TO BE GREEN

WOMAN 4:
MY MAMA SAID

WOMAN 4 (CONT'D):

YOU MUST BE POLITE
BUT SOMETIMES
YOUR GIFTS JUST AIN'T RIGHT
I REALLY TRY
TO FIGURE IT OUT
JUST WHAT WERE YOU THINKING ABOUT
THEY SAY THAT THE
THOUGHT IS WHAT COUNTS
TRY NOT TO FOCUS
ON DOLLAR AMOUNTS
BUT WHEN IT'S SOMETHIN'
I JUST CAN'T ACCEPT
I'M GONNA REGIFT
ON THAT YOU CAN BET

WOMAN 1, 2, 3:

AND DO THE REGIFT!

WOMAN 4:

COULD BE A SWEATER WITH CATS

WOMAN 1, 2, 3:

DO THE REGIFT

WOMAN 4:

A HAT WITH BEER MUGS ATTACHED

WOMAN 1, 2, 3:

DO THE REGIFT

WOMAN 4:

SLIPPERS THAT LOOK LIKE PIGS

WOMAN 1, 2, 3:

DO THE REGIFT

WOMAN 4:

A BRAND-NEW MULLET WIG
IT WAS UNDER THE CHRISTMAS TREE
I WONDERED WHAT IT COULD BE
IT WAS FROM THE MAN I LOVE
I'M SURE IT WAS SENT FROM ABOVE
BUT ALAS ON CHRISTMAS DAY
ALL MY DREAMS WERE DASHED AWAY
OPENED IT UP IT DIDN'T THRILL
IT WAS THE NEW GEORGE FOREMAN GRILL

WOMAN 1, 2, 3:

AND DO THE REGIFT!

WOMAN 4:
A FLASHING LIGHT UP NECKLACE

WOMAN 1, 2, 3:
DO THE REGIFT

WOMAN 4:
A BARKING DOG THAT CAN FLIP

WOMAN 1, 2, 3:
DO THE REGIFT

WOMAN 4:
FIGURINE FOR YOUR HOME

WOMAN 1, 2, 3:
THE REGIFT

WOMAN 4:
A FANCY GARDEN GNOME

WOMAN 4:
IF IT DOESN'T COME WITH A RECIEPT
IT'S THE REGIFT YOU JUST CAN NOT BEAT
INSTEAD OF IT LYING AROUND
PASS IT ALL OVER TOWN

WOMAN 1, 2, 3:
STEP ONE:

WOMAN 4:
THE SUPRISE

WOMAN 1, 2, 3:
STEP TWO:

WOMAN 4:
A BIG FAKE SMILE

WOMAN 1, 2, 3:
STEP THREE:

WOMAN 4:
SOME GRATITUDE

WOMAN 1, 2, 3:
STEP FOUR:

WOMAN 4:
DON'T BE RUDE

WOMAN 1, 2, 3:
STEP FIVE:

WOMAN 4:
YOU GOTTA TAKE IT HOME

WOMAN 1, 2, 3:
STEP SIX:

WOMAN 4:
YOU BETTER LEAVE IT ALONE

WOMAN 1, 2, 3:
STEP SEVEN:

WOMAN 4:
IT'S A HOLIDAY

WOMAN 1, 2, 3:
STEP EIGHT:

WOMAN 4:
YOU CAN GIVE IT AWAY

WOMAN 1, 2, 3:
AND DO THE REGIFT!

WOMAN 4::
A THING DON'T WANT TO OWN

WOMAN 1, 2, 3:
DO THE REGIFT

WOMAN 4:
FIND IT A BRAND-NEW HOME

WOMAN 1, 2, 3:
DO THE REGIFT

WOMAN 4:
YOU'RE NOT BEING MEAN

WOMAN 1, 2, 3:
DO THE REGIFT

WOMAN 4:
IT'S GOOD TO BE GREEN

WOMAN 1, 2, 3:
DO THE REGIFT

WOMAN 4:
RECYCLING IS THE BEST

WOMAN 1, 2, 3:
DO THE REGIFT

WOMAN 4:
AND YOU'LL SAVE THE PLANET

WOMAN 1, 2, 3:
DO THE REGIFT

WOMAN 4:
MAMA SAID DO NOT WASTE

WOMAN 1, 2, 3:
DO THE REGIFT
YOU SEE THERE IS NO DEBATE

ALL:
JUST DO THE REGIFT!

WOMAN 2: "He put a ring in the toe of a stocking. On Christmas Eve, we opened our stockings and it was there at the bottom of the toe.

WOMAN 2 (CONT'D): Then he got down on his knees and he was shaking." –A quote from actress Kyra Sedgwick on her hunky husband Kevin Bacon, Made-for-TV GRITS!

WOMAN 1: When we think of the holidays, there is usually a special Christmas that comes to mind first. For me, it was my first Christmas as a married woman just last year.

We were married on November 21st so everything and I mean everything was truly brand new. We still had our own apartments and were building a tiny house in a new development in Charlotte, North Carolina. All we wanted was to be together, but it would seem that all everyone else wanted was for us to be with them. You know how that is. First Christmas as a married couple, who will go where, when and how? It can be quite traumatic! All a new couple wants to do is make everyone happy that first holiday season and after it, they realize that that is impossible to do. So, you make choices and compromise and life changes and moves on, but not that first Christmas.

I'll set up the travel itinerary for ya.

WOMAN 1 rushes from SR to SL back and forth during her "travel."

FIRST: Christmas Eve, we went to Monroe, North Carolina ('cause that's what HIS family ALWAYS did). SECOND-We hopped a red-Eye to Jacksonville, Florida where my parents lived so we could be there on Christmas day (cause that's what MY family ALWAYS did). And THIRD: we flew back Christmas night so we could hop in the car and drive to travel to Rockingham North Carolina to be with his extended family AND celebrate his grandmother's 84th birthday which, of course, fell exactly on December 26th.

WELL... December 27th, we drug ourselves through the front door of my tiny apartment LATE that night and plopped down on my rickety ole sofa and collapsed. The 72-hour holiday express! Even though we were exhausted, we were ...happy. We had made it through the ordeal with our marriage still intact. And I think we only had one... *(Pause)* hundred arguments that holiday.

We looked at the pitiful three-foot Christmas tree by the fireplace covered with ornaments we received as weddings gifts and smiled. Well at least now we can have OUR Christmas.

WOMAN 1: As the words "Merry Christmas Charlotte" came out of my new husband's mouth, the very expensive Christopher Radko ornament that we had received for our wedding exploded into a million pieces. Why? We still don't know to this day! I burst into tears, then hysterical laughter. He just looked at me and said, "Honey, we won't do it this way next year. I promise. This is our life now." I realized he was right. I know now that I never really knew what the holidays were all about until I got to share them with him. I never really knew life until him.

WOMAN 1 moves to SR or SL tree. She finds her favorite ornament. She sings this song while looking at the ornament and finally replaces upon the tree.

SONG #5: *I NEVER KNEW LIFE WITHOUT YOU*

WOMAN 1 (CONT'D):

YOU CAME INTO MY LIFE
A SWEET UNANSWERED PRAYER
I COULD HAVE BLINKED MY EYES
AND MISSED WHEN YOU WEREN'T THERE
NOW I SEE THIS LIFE
IS BRAND NEW
I NEVER KNEW LIFE WITHOUT YOU

NO PROBLEM IS TOO MUCH
FOR YOUR UNJUDGING EARS
NO HURT I CANNOT SHARE
YOU'LL WIPE AWAY MY TEARS
THERE'S NOTHING FOR YOU
I WOULDN'T DO
I NEVER KNEW LIFE WITHOUT YOU
CHORUS
WHO WAS I BEFORE
YOU OPENED MY EYES
I WAS WALKING THROUGH LIFE
ALL ALONE
WHERE DID I LIVE
THAT STREET WITH NO NAME
YOU MADE MY SAD HEART
HAVE A HOME

WAS THERE A TIME
I DID NOT KNOW YOUR NAME?
OR CARRY YOUR SONG
IN MY HEART?
I THINK THAT MY LIFE
WAS AN UNFINISHED PLAY
'TIL YOU TOOK THE LEADING PART!

WOMAN 1 (CONT'D):

I FOUND SOMETHING THAT I
NEVER KNEW
I THANK THE LORD ABOVE
FOR SENDING ME TO YOU
I KNOW THAT WITH YOUR LOVE
THERE'S NOTHING I CAN'T DO
I NEVER KNEW LIFE WITHOUT YOU
I NEVER KNEW LIFE WITHOUT YOU
I NEVER KNEW LIFE... WITHOUT YOU

WOMAN 4: "Do not ever give a Queen a home appliance as a gift. Period. The End."– A quote from Miss Jill Conner Brown, Author of The Sweet Potato Queen Book Serie: Tupelo, Mississippi GRITS!

WOMAN 2: Now listen. I know that Christmas is a time of family and celebrating our blessings. I know that there is nothing better than sharing with those that you love. I know that we must be thankful and grateful for all that we receive. SO, what I am about to say, I say in the most loving and caring way that I know how.

There are SOME members of the family, that for as long as I shall live, I will NEVER, NEVER, NEVER, NEVER, NEVER, understand! Y'all know who I'm talking about. She comes every Christmas bearing gifts. She's unassuming, kind and yes, a little weird. She's your crazy aunt. Don't laugh. We all have one. Heck, you may even BE one. But rest assured, she's comin', and on December 25th, when you open her gift you are gonna wish that you were one of those high stakes poker players with a fool proof bluff. That's right. It's gonna be the department store free gift with purchase for you or the hand painted canvas with the wolves on a snowy day. It could be a cookie jar, with a couple of cracks and crumbs in the bottom that she found at a garage sale. And listen it don't matter whether you been naughty or nice. You are gonna get it and you are definitely gonna think twice.

I remember back in the 80s my crazy Aunt Barbara from Florida found a "great deal" on "Members Only" jackets... y'all remember those? So cool, right? She got one for every member of the family, in all different colors. Problem was these were "Crazy Aunt" jackets. In fact, they weren't even "Members Only" jackets at all. No, no, no! These were "MOMBERS Only" jackets. The tag sewn onto the front was misspelled! Totally awesome, dude.

My friend Donna from Virginia got a REAL special gift. It was close to her heart... literally. She and her sisters all received the ever popular "dickies" from their crazy aunt. Popular in 1973... but y'all to crazy aunts those gifts are timeless!

Bless their hearts. They mean well don't they, but every Christmas it's the same. The gift under the tree that's misshapen, leaking, smelling weird, moving on its own or wrapped in happy birthday paper is gonna be real special, just like that aunt.

WOMAN 2 (CONT'D): And that's ok; now every December 25th, I just know I'm gonna have to deal with the Crazy Aunt Free Gift with Purchase Garage Sale Christmastime Blues.

SONG #6: THE CRAZY AUNT BLUES

(Singing)

I'M GONNA CRY
CRY ALL SEASON LONG
OH YOU'LL MAKE ME CRY
CRY ALL SEASON LONG
CAUSE YOU RSVP'ED
AND ARE STANDIN' AT MY DOOR

OH I LOVE YOU
BUT YOU ALWAYS DO ME WRONG
AT CHRISTMASTIME
YOU'RE ALWAYS TREATING ME WRONG
STRANGE STRANGE GIFTS OF LOVE
AND THAT'S WHY I'M SINGING THIS SONG

YOU LOOK SO SWEET
BUT I KNOW WHERE YOU BEEN
OH YEAH YOU LOOK SO SWEET
BUT I KNOW WHERE YOU BEEN
HANGIN' IN THE THRIFT STORE
SIFTIN' THROUGH THE BARGAIN BIN

YOU LOOK JUST LIKE
YOU HANDED ME SOME GOLD
APPRECIATE
YOUR BLESSINGS I AM TOLD
BUT THIS FRUITCAKE HERE
EXPIRED OVER TWO YEARS AGO!

WOMAN 2 enters the audience and finds some "crazy" aunts! House lights up, and if spot is available, follow Woman 2 to each "crazy aunt."

I KNOW YOU LOVE
LOVE THE DOLLAR STORE
YES, I KNOW YOU LOVE

WOMAN 2 (CONT'D):

THE DOLLAR TREE, JUST A DOLLAR, DOLLAR GENERAL, EVERYTHING'S A DOLLAR AND THE NINETY-NINE CENT STORE

BUT I JUST CAN'T TAKE IT

TAKE IT ANYMORE

OH, I HAVE GOT THE CRAZY AUNT BLUES

SO, BLESS HER HEART AND LETS ALL SPREAD THE NEWS

ABOUT THE CRAZY AUNT BLUES

WOMAN 1, 3, 4:

CRAZY AUNT BLUES

WOMAN 2:

I DON'T GET THE CRAZY AUNT BLUES

WOMAN 1, 3, 4:

CRAZY AUNT BLUES

WOMAN 2:

YOU BETTER WATCH YOURSELF OR SHE MIGHT JUST GET YOU TOO.

I GOT THE CRAZY AUNT BLUES

WOMAN 1, 3, 4:

CRAZY AUNT BLUES

WOMAN 2:

OH YEAH, THE CRAZY AUNT BLUES

WOMAN 1, 3, 4:

CRAZY AUNT BLUES

WOMAN 2:

OH YEAH, SHE'S COMIN' FOR YOU

WOMAN 1, 3, 4:

COMIN' FOR YOU

WOMAN 2:

AND NOT A THING YOU CAN DO

WOMAN 1, 3, 4:

NOTHIN' TO DO

WOMAN 2:

TO LOSE THE FREE GIFT WITH PURCHASE, GARAGE SALE CRAZY AUNT BLUES!

WOMAN 3: "Nothing says holidays like a cheese log." Miss Ellen DeGeneres, Louisiana GRITS!

WOMAN 2: For hundreds of thousands of Southerners, a Christmas feast means turkey and dressin', cranberries and sweet potato casserole, but for some, Christmas means the well-spiced chicken and meat dishes of Latin Texas. Or maybe it's the North Carolina Moravian "love feasts" of coffee and buns and lighted candles in the hands of participants.

WOMAN 3: The Southern holidays are as steeped in tradition and custom as a Virginia mince pie is in spirits!

WOMAN 4: Many of our sweet Christmas goodies are quite possibly versions of a recipe that was handed down by Martha Washington. It was Martha's directions on her Old Dominion's "Great Cake" that began "Take forty eggs..." Today people are still taking forty eggs, or fractions thereof, and following Martha's rules!

WOMAN 3: Eggnog is said to have been made popular in the United States by none other than her husband, George, in which he used both rye and Jamaican rum and a generous dollop of mellow sherry for good measure and good fumes! The gentlemen of Richmond, Roanoke and Charlottesville still emulate him today with that same formula *(Hiccup)* or so I'm told!

WOMAN 1: Whether your holiday meal consists of spice or spirits, poultry or pies, any Southerner will tell you that the season just wouldn't be the same without its culinary treasures. It's those traditions that bring us all together around a table each year. A blessed time to gather and celebrate. Visit any old country home or mountain retreat during holiday mealtime and you're likely to hear one of the oldest toasts in the south.

ALL raise their hands in a toast.

ALL: "All our friends."

Over musical intro, ALL move to bring out a table filled with the food items mentioned in the song, all in a row, in the order they are presented musically. They improv about being hungry, "What did you make?," "Ooh this looks good!," etc. Each woman will hold up her item each time she sings about it during the song. It looks like a busy line of activity as each woman moves behind the other to get to her item. WOMAN 3 slowly gets drunk from singing about and eating the "bourbon balls" each verse. The ladies are surprised and slightly frustrated with her. By the end she is quite tipsy singing about the sweet tea, because she has found the bottle of bourbon in the bourbon ball tin and puts it into the sweet tea! The other gals usher her off at the end of the song as she is still talking and has a hiccup at the end.

SONG #7: 12 YUMMY DAYS OF CHRISTMAS

WOMAN 3:

ON THE FIRST DAY OF CHRISTMAS MY FAMILY RECEIVED

A GALLON OF SWEET TEA

WOMAN 2:

ON THE SECOND DAY OF CHRISTMAS MY FAMILY RECEIVED

TWO HAM BISCUITS

WOMAN 3:
AND A GALLON OF SWEET TEA

WOMAN 1:
ON THE THIRD DAY OF CHRISTMAS MY FAMILY RECEIVED
THREE POUND CAKES

WOMAN 2:
TWO HAM BISCUITS

WOMAN 3:
AND A GALLON OF SWEET TEA

WOMAN 4:
ON THE FOURTH DAY OF CHRISTMAS MY FAMILY RECEIVED
FOUR PECAN PIES

WOMAN 1:
THREE POUND CAKES

WOMAN 2:
TWO HAM BISCUITS

WOMAN 3:
AND A GALLON OF SWEET TEA
ON THE FIFTH DAY OF CHRISTMAS MY FAMILY RECEIVED
FIVE BOURBON BALLS

WOMAN 4:
FOUR PECAN PIES

WOMAN 1:
THREE POUND CAKES

WOMAN 2:
TWO HAM BISCUITS

WOMAN 3:
AND A GALLON OF SWEET TEA

WOMAN 2:
ON THE SIXTH DAY OF CHRISTMAS MY FAMILY RECEIVED
SIX AMBROSIA SALADS

WOMAN 3:
FIVE BOURBON BALLS

WOMAN 4:
FOUR PECAN PIES

WOMAN 1:
THREE POUND CAKES

WOMAN 2:
TWO HAM BISCUITS

WOMAN 3:
AND A GALLON OF SWEET TEA

WOMAN 1:
ON THE SEVENTH DAY OF CHRISTMAS MY FAMILY RECEIVED
SEVEN GOLDEN TURKEYS

WOMAN 2:
SIX AMBROSIA SALADS

WOMAN 3:
FIVE BOURBON BALLS

WOMAN 4:
FOUR PECAN PIES

WOMAN 1:
THREE POUND CAKES

WOMAN 2:
TWO HAM BISCUITS

WOMAN 3:
AND A GALLON OF SWEET TEA

WOMAN 4:
ON THE EIGHTH DAY OF CHRISTMAS MY FAMILY RECEIVED
EIGHT JARS OF CHOW CHOW

WOMAN 1:
SEVEN GOLDEN TURKEYS

WOMAN 2:
SIX AMBROSIA SALADS

WOMAN 3:
FIVE POUNDS BOURBON BALLS

WOMAN 4:
FOUR PECAN PIES

WOMAN 1:
THREE POUND CAKES

WOMAN 2:
TWO HAM BISCUITS

WOMAN 3:
AND A GALLON OF SWEET TEA
ON THE NINTH DAY OF CHRISTMAS MY FAMILY RECEIVED
NINE POUNDS OF COLLARDS

WOMAN 4:
EIGHT JARS OF CHOW CHOW

WOMAN 1:
SEVEN GOLDEN TURKEYS

WOMAN 2:
SIX AMBROSIA SALADS

WOMAN 3:
FIVE BOURBON BALLS

WOMAN 4:
FOUR PECAN PIES

WOMAN 1:
THREE POUND CAKES

WOMAN 2:
TWO HAM BISCUITS

WOMAN 3:
AND A GALLON OF SWEET TEA

WOMAN 2:
ON THE TENTH DAY OF CHRISTMAS MY FAMILY RECEIVED
TEN MOON PIES

WOMAN 3:
NINE POUNDS OF COLLARDS

WOMAN 4:
EIGHT JARS OF CHOW CHOW

WOMAN 1:
SEVEN GOLDEN TURKEYS

WOMAN 2:
SIX AMBROSIA SALADS

WOMAN 3:
FIVE BOURBON BALLS

WOMAN 4:
FOUR PECAN PIES

WOMAN 1:
THREE POUND CAKES

WOMAN 2:
TWO HAM BISCUITS

WOMAN 3:
AND A GALLON OF SWEET TEA

WOMAN 1:
ON THE ELEVENTH DAY OF CHRISTMAS MY FAMILY RECEIVED
ELEVEN DEVILED EGGS

WOMAN 2:
TEN MOON PIES

WOMAN 3:
NINE POUNDS OF COLLARDS

WOMAN 4:
EIGHT JARS OF CHOW CHOW

WOMAN 1:
SEVEN GOLDEN TURKEYS

WOMAN 2:
SIX AMBROSIA SALADS

WOMAN 3:
FIVE BOURBON BALLS

WOMAN 4:
FOUR PECAN PIES

WOMAN 1:
THREE POUND CAKES

WOMAN 2:
TWO HAM BISCUITS

WOMAN 3:
AND A GALLON OF SWEET TEA

WOMAN 4:
ON THE TWELFTH DAY OF CHRISTMAS MY FAMILY RECEIVED
TWELVE FRIED CHICKEN LEGS

WOMAN 1:
ELEVEN DEVILED EGGS

WOMAN 2:
TEN MOON PIES

WOMAN 3:
NINE POUNDS OF COLLARDS

WOMAN 4:
EIGHT JARS OF CHOW CHOW

WOMAN 1:
SEVEN GOLDEN TURKEYS

WOMAN 2:
SIX AMBROSIA SALADS

WOMAN 3:
FIVE BOURBON BALLS

WOMAN 4:
FOUR PECAN PIES

WOMAN 1:
THREE POUND CAKES

WOMAN 2:
TWO HAM BISCUITS

WOMAN 3:
AND A GALLON OF SWEET TEA

END ACT I

ACT II

WOMAN 3: "When Christmas bells are swinging above the fields of snow, we hear sweet voices ringing from lands of long ago. And etched on vacant places, are half-forgotten faces, of friends we used to cherish, and loves we used to know." –A poem called "Christmas Fancies" by Miss Ella Wheeler Wilcox, honorary purty talkin' GRITS from Wisconsin!

ALL enter wearing hoop skirt slips that are decorated in garland, bells, and bows. They have large Christmas bow hats or headbands. The bells on the skirt shake as they enter. They treat the skirts like the bottom of a bell and they are the clapper underneath swinging their skirts to make the bells "ring" comically.

WOMAN 2: Christmas bells have always been an important part of the Southern holiday season. Whether you are ringing with your bell choir at church, jingling them with your neighborhood carolers or just hanging them on your front door, a true Southern woman will always bring out her bells for the holidays.

WOMAN 1: But Georgia... you left out the most important belles of all! Southern Belles! Why there are even songs dedicated to us women who make this most special of all holidays a thing of beauty and excess!

WOMAN 2: Of course, wait... what?

WOMAN 4: Songs about us?

WOMAN 1: Oh yes... why there's that song "Silver Belles" ...about our sisters who bring out that precious sterling flatware for special holiday meals...

WOMAN 4: Honey, I don't think that's what that song is about...

WOMAN 1: And that beautiful piece, "Carol of the Belles!" That's the one about my sorority sister Carol... of the prestigious Belle family in Birmingham. Oooh! They throw THE most extravagant parties during the holidays.

WOMAN 3: Charlotte, carol is a song.

WOMAN 1: Yes, I know! She weaves decorations and music and food together like a perfectly written symphony!

WOMAN 2: Oh my... I think she's confused.

WOMAN 1: And what about that Christmas song about all the money we raise for charity during the holidays? We have all that change makin noise in our buckets and pockets and bags!

WOMAN 3: Which one is that?

WOMAN 1: Why "Jingle Belles" of course!

ALL react in disbelief and irritation.

WOMAN 2: Girls... I think it would be best... for everyone... if we stop DISCUSSING bells and start SINGING about them! What do ya say?!

SONG #8: *BELLE MEDLEY- (CAROLING, CAROLING/CAROL OF THE BELLS/SILVER BELLS)*

WOMAN 1, 2, 4:
DING DONG DING DONG CHRISTMAS BELLS ARE RINGING

WOMAN 3:
CAROLING, CAROLING NOW WE GO

WOMAN 1, 2, 4:
CHRISTMAS BELLS ARE RINGING

WOMAN 3:
CAROLING, CAROLING THROUGH THE SNOW

WOMAN 1, 2, 4:
CHRISTMAS BELLS ARE RINGING

WOMAN 3:
JOYOUS VOICES SWEET AND CLEAR, SING THE SAD-OF-HEART TO CHEER

ALL:
DING DONG DING DONG CHRISTMAS BELLS ARE RINGING

WOMAN 1:
CAROLING CAROLING THROUGH THE TOWN

WOMAN 2, 3, 4:
CHRISTMAS BELLS ARE RINGING

WOMAN 1:
CAROLING CAROLING UP AND DOWN

WOMAN 2, 3, 4:
CHRISTMAS BELLS ARE RINGING

WOMAN 1:
SING WE ALL THIS HAPPY MORN, NOW THE KING OF HEAVEN IS BORN

ALL:
DING DONG DING DONG CHRISTMAS BELLS ARE RINGING

DING DONG DING DONG CHRISTMAS BELLS ARE RINGING!

WOMAN 3:
HARK HOW THE BELLS, SWEET SILVER BELLS, ALL SEEM TO SAY, THROW CARES AWAY

CHRISTMAS IS HERE BRINGING GOOD CHEER TO YOUNG AND OLD, MEEK AND THE BOLD

WOMAN 1:
DING DONG DING DONG THAT IS THEIR SONG WITH JOYFUL RING ALL CAROLING

ONE SEEMS TO HEAR WORDS OF GOOD CHEER FROM EVERYWHERE FILLING THE AIR

OH HOW THEY POUND RAISING THE SOUND OR HILL AND DALE TELLING THE TALE

ALL:

GAILY THEY RING WHILE PEOPLE SING SONGS OF GOOD CHEER
CHRISTMAS IS HERE

WOMAN 1, 3:

MERRY MERRY MERRY CHRISTMAS

MERRY MERRY MERRY CHRISTMAS

WOMAN 3:

ON HOW THEY SEND ON WITHOUT END

WOMAN 1:

THIER JOYFUL TONE TO EVERY HOME

WOMAN 3:

HARK HOW THE BELLS SWEET SILVER BELLS

WOMAN 1:

ALL SEEM TO SAY THROW CARES AWAY

ALL:

DING DONG DING DONG

WOMAN 4:

CITY SIDEWALKS BUSY SIDEWALKS DRESSED IN HOLIDAY STYLE

IN THE AIR THERE'S A FEELING OF CHRISTMAS

CHILDREN LAUGHING PEOPLE PASSING MEETING SMILE AFTER SMILE

AND ON EVERY STREET CORNER YOU'LL HEAR

SILVER BELLS

WOMAN 1, 2, 3:

SILVER BELLS

WOMAN 4:

SILVER BELLS

WOMAN 1, 2, 3:

SILVER BELLS

WOMAN 4:

IT'S CHRISTMAS TIME IN THE CITY

WOMAN 1, 2, 3:

IT'S CHRISTMAS TIME IN THE CITY

WOMAN 4:

RING A LING

WOMAN 1, 2, 3:

RING A LING

WOMAN 4:

HEAR THEM RING

WOMAN 1, 2, 3:

HEAR THEM RING

WOMAN 4:

SOON IT WILL BE CHRISTMAS DAY

WOMAN 2:
CITY STREETLIGHTS, EVEN STOP LIGHTS BLINK A BRIGHT RED AND GREEN
AS THE SHOPPERS RUSH HOME WITH THIER TREASURES
HEAR THE SNOW CRUNCH, SEE THE KIDS BUNCH THIS IS SANTA'S BIG SCENE
AND ABOVE ALL THE BUSTLE YOU WILL HEAR
SILVER BELLS

WOMAN 1, 2, 3:
SILVER BELLS

WOMAN 4:
SILVER BELLS

WOMAN 1, 2, 3:
SILVER BELLS

WOMAN 4:
IT'S CHRISTMAS TIME IN THE CITY

WOMAN 1, 2, 3:
IT'S CHRISTMAS TIME IN THE CITY

WOMAN 4:
RING A LING

WOMAN 1, 2, 3:
RING A LING

WOMAN 4:
HEAR THEM RING

WOMAN 1, 2, 3:
HEAR THEM RING
SOON IT WILL BE CHRISTMAS DAY
SOON IT WILL BE CHRISTMAS DAY

ALL:
SOON IT WILL BE CHRISTMAS DAY!

WOMAN 3: "I wondered about Santa Claus when I was six. Mother took me to see him in a department store and he asked for my autograph!" –A quote from Miss Shirley Temple, Hollywood GRITS!

WOMAN 1: Christmas is a time of wonder. One year, I remember I was about six or seven and I was starting to "wonder" about the reality of Old Saint Nick. My grandmother sat me down in her favorite comfy chair and pulled a very old manila envelope from the antique cedar chest in the living room. I watched her carefully pull out a yellowing piece of newspaper that was folded in half.

She pulls out a piece of yellowing newspaper from off of the fireplace mantel.

She told me it belonged to my great-grandmother. She was in the newspaper when she was just about my age.

WOMAN 1 (CONT'D): I was intrigued by such a grown-up achievement from such a little girl. I asked Nana what it said. She said that her mom wondered about Santa Claus too and she thought the best place to find out about him was from the folks that gave out information to the world on a daily basis back then... the newspaper. Nana delicately unfolded the paper and began to read.

WOMAN 1 unfolds the paper and reads this story.

It said,

"We take pleasure in answering you in the communication below, expressing at the same time our great gratification that its author is among the friends of The Sun Tribune." Great-grandma had written this:

"Dear Editor— I am 8 years old. Some of my friends say there is no Santa Claus. Papa says, 'If you see it in The Sun, it is so.' Please tell me the truth, is there a Santa Claus?"

Mary Ann O'Hanlon,

115 West Church Street

The reply read:

"Mary Ann, your little friends are wrong. They have been affected by the skepticism of a skeptical age. They do not believe in anything they cannot see.

Yes, Virginia, there is a Santa Claus. He exists as certainly as love and generosity exist. Alas! How dreary would the world be if there were no Santa Claus! It would be as dreary as if there were no Mary Anns.

The most real things in the world are those that neither children nor men can see. No Santa Claus! Thank God! He lives, and he lives forever. A thousand years from now, Virginia, nay, ten times ten thousand years from now, he will continue to make glad the heart of childhood."

Then Nana put the paper down and smiled at me. It was like she was hearing the story for the first time. I asked her what she was smiling about and she said she was thinking about what a fine woman her mother was and how I was so much like her. It was nice knowing that my great grandmother had had doubts too. I was so thankful that I didn't have to spend that Christmas wondering about Old Saint Nick. I knew he was coming down the chimney for sure. After all, like my great grandpapa said if you see it in "The Sun", it is so!

SONG #9: YES, THERE IS A SANTA CLAUS

ALL WOMEN do choreography together in this piece. Sassy dancing using candy canes as dancing canes and wearing oversized Santa hats.

WOMAN 1 (CONT'D):

HE'S THE MAN WITH THE BAG AND OLD SAINT NICK
HE CAN FLY UP THE CHIMNEY WITH A GRIN AND A WINK
A LEGEND, FOLKLORE, A TIME-OLD TALE
BUT HE'S REAL TO ME, STILL THE SAME

THE NOTES TO HIM I WRITE EACH YEAR
AND AT CHRISTMASTIME I KNOW HE HEARS
THE DREAMS OF CHILDREN FAR AND NEAR
OF PRECIOUS TREASURES HELD SO DEAR

ALL:

SO YES THERE IS A SANTA CLAUS
HE LIVES WITHIN MY HEART
NOT TIME NOR SPACE CAN ERR REPLACE
THE FEELING THAT HE STARTS
ANTICIPATE, FACILITATE EXCITEMENT ALL AROUND
THE COMING AND THE DREAMING OF THE GIFTS YET TO BE FOUND
HE IS THE ONE THAT I DREAM OF
THE WHOLE HOLIDAY TIME
SO YES, THERE IS A SANTA CLAUS
HE LIVES WITHIN MY MIND!

WOMAN 1:

CLOSE YOUR EYES AND YOU CAN SEE
HIM STANDING THERE, REALITY
DON'T LET IT GO, IT'S MAGICAL
LIKE BEING WITH THE ONES YOU LOVE
A PART OF YOU, A PART OF ME
HIS NAME WILL LIVE, ETERNALLY
IT'S NOT TOO LATE TO JUST BELIEVE
IN ALL THE THINGS YOU CANNOT SEE

ALL:

SO YES THERE IS A SANTA CLAUS
HE LIVES WITHIN MY HEART
NOT TIME NOR SPACE CAN ERR REPLACE
THE FEELING THAT HE STARTS
ANTICIPATE, FACILITATE EXCITEMENT ALL AROUND
THE COMING AND THE DREAMING OF THE GIFTS YET TO BE FOUND
HE IS THE ONE THAT I DREAM OF
THE WHOLE HOLIDAY TIME
SO YES, THERE IS A SANTA CLAUS
HE LIVES WITHIN MY MIND!

WOMAN 1:

REMEMBER THAT YOU'RE NOT TOO OLD
RECALL THE STORIES YOU WERE TOLD
RECEIVE THE GIFT THAT CAN'T BE BOUGHT
RESIST LOGICAL WAY OF THOUGHT!
THE WONDER OF THAT TIME OF YEAR
OF RINGING BELLS, WE LOVE TO HEAR
OF SNOWY DAYS AND BLINKING LIGHTS
OF WARM EMBRACES HELD SO TIGHT
OF MUSIC SOFT, MEMORIES CLEAR
OF TWINKLY EYES, A LONG WHITE BEARD
SUGARPLUMS INSIDE YOUR HEAD
NOW SAY A PRAYER THEN OFF TO BED

ALL:

'CAUSE YES THERE IS A SANTA CLAUS
HE LIVES WITHIN MY HEART
NOT TIME NOR SPACE CAN ERR REPLACE
THE FEELING THAT HE STARTS
ANTICIPATE, FACILITATE EXCITEMENT ALL AROUND
THE COMING AND THE DREAMING OF THE GIFTS YET TO BE FOUND
HE IS THE ONE THAT I DREAM OF
THE WHOLE HOLIDAY TIME
SO YES, THERE IS A SANTA CLAUS
HE LIVES WITHIN MY MIND!
SO YES, THERE IS A SANTA CLAUS
HE LIVES WITHIN MY MIND!

WOMAN 4: "The one thing women don't want to find in their stockings on Christmas morning is their husband." –Miss Joan Rivers, God rest her soul... Artificial GRITS!

WOMAN 2: My husband, bless his heart, has never been an interior decorator sort of guy. In fact most of his passions, other than me of course, lie outside of the home. He's a hangout in the woods, fly-fishin', amber liquid drinkin', football watchin' attorney. So, when he brought home a faux Christmas tree for our new house in Charleston, South Carolina, I suppose I should have been thrilled with the effort alone. This on-sale, Big Lots lookin' tree was, shall we say, sparse in foliage and our new Georgia plantation-style home hosted gracious 16-foot ceilings. This "Charlie Brown tree" was simply not going to do. What would our new Carolinian neighbors think? That's just NOT how you do a Carolina Christmas on the coast!

Unbeknownst to him, the next day I took it upon myself to buy us a "proper" tree. It was *(Pause, recalling)* ...large, but the two burly lot workers seemed to have no trouble hoisting it a top the Blazer and strapping it down.

WOMAN 2 (CONT'D): No matter it hung three feet over both the front and the back of the vehicle, it was THE one! I had a little bit of trouble pulling it into the garage and I guess my husband heard the commotion, because not long after my attempted entry, he appeared.

All he said was, "This is... BIG." What proceeded from that moment on would be MY favorite and my HUSBAND'S worst all-time memories of the Christmas holiday.

As soon as the bungee cords snapped, the tree was on the garage floor. The trunk was SO big that it wouldn't even fit into its fancy base, so my husband commenced to hacking it furiously with a machete so that it could be wedged into the stand. Wood chips and pine needles were flyin' through the air, many of which stuck to his clothes and face, both of which were eventually covered in sap.

By the time he dragged the enormous tree through the not-so-enormous door frame, numerous braches had broken off, the door frame was significantly damaged and he had so many pine needles stuck to him that he looked like a deranged porcupine! As I watched from the comfy sidelines, I did the only helpful thing I could do. I began to laugh. This did not help.

He chopped two feet of the top of the tree with his busted-up machete like he was Indiana Jones on an expedition through the Amazon jungle. Finally, the tree was set up in the corner. I decided it was best NOT to ask him to light the darn thing so I began with a very tall ladder and five strands of lights, which only covered about one third of the tree. Approximately three trips to the Walgreens later, we had enough lights to illuminate the whole tree and possibly the neighborhood. By this time, my sweet man, still sap-covered— was well into a fifth of bourbon and laughing. The thing was so big and bright it looked like the Morris Island lighthouse.

All in all, the ordeal required one very long shower, some new door trim, an upgrade to our electrical system and the sweeping out of two tons of wood chips from our home. But y'all, it was the prettiest tree we ever had. So big and bright that I am sure planes passing by thought we were an airstrip. Perfect. Just the kind of subtle classy Christmas that only the Carolinas can provide!

SONG #10: CAROLINA CHRISTMAS

OTHER LADIES may join in on harmony during the chorus if desired. WOMAN 2 sits on her stool or in a chair for V1 and moves to gather the ladies together as the song continues in a conversational manner until they all arrive under one of the Christmas trees together as a group of friends celebrating. Drinks may be held. Ornaments may be moved around on tree as if they are decorating it.

WOMAN 2 (CONT'D):

I'VE BEEN TO A LOT OF PLACES
SEEN A LOT OF THINGS
MISSED MY HOME MORE THAN A TIME OR TWO
BEEN ACROSS THE SEA
DONE SOME TRAVELIN'
DISCOVERED MY FAIR SHARE OF TRUTH
BUT I KNOW FOR SURE
THAT THE PLACE I LOVE
IS THE PLACE THAT I KNOW BEST
THE ONLY PLACE
I CAN FIND SOME PEACE
LAY DOWN MY HEAD AND REST

OCEAN AND SAND
SNOW AND MOUNTAINS
BLINKIN' LIGHTS ON AN OLD PALM TREE
COLD OR WARM
AN OLD COUNTRY FARM
SAWGRASS OR SNOW COVERED LEAVES
Y'ALL COME ON DOWN
AND HEAR THE SOUNDS
OF WHAT FAMILY AND FREINDS LOVE BEST
YOU'LL FIT RIGHT IN
NO MATTER WHERE YOU BEEN
THAT'S A CAROLINA CHRISTMAS

IT'S THE LAND WE KNOW
THE LAND SO GRAND
THEY GAVE IT NORTH AND SOUTH
AND AT CHRISTMASTIME
I OFTEN FIND
IT'S ALL I DREAM ABOUT
BY THE FIRELIGHT
OR WALKIN' ON THE BEACH
I KNOW MY SPIRIT WILL BE
WISHIN THAT THE ONES
I LOVE THE MOST
COULD BE RIGHT HERE WITH ME

WOMAN 2 (CONT'D):

OCEAN AND SAND
SNOW AND MOUNTAINS
BLINKIN' LIGHTS ON AN OLD PALM TREE
COLD OR WARM
AN OLD COUNTRY FARM
SAWGRASS OR SNOW-COVERED LEAVES
Y'ALL COME ON DOWN
AND HEAR THE SOUNDS
OF WHAT FAMILY AND FREINDS LOVE BEST
YOU'LL FIT RIGHT IN
NO MATTER WHERE YOU BEEN
THAT'S A CAROLINA CHRISTMAS

LITTLE THINGS THAT COUNT
THAT'S WHAT WE'RE ALL ABOUT
THAT'S A CAROLINA CHRISTMAS
THAT'S A CAROLINA CHRISTMAS
THAT'S A CAROLINA CHRISTMAS

WOMAN 1: "Which Christmas is the most vivid to me? It's always the next Christmas." –Miss Joanne Woodward, American film actress and Georgia GRITS

WOMAN 4: Bonjour y'all! You know, I come from a long line of Mademoiselles from Vicksburg. A town perched right above the Mississippi river, a town that thrived with river country touches. My family remembers the holiday's way back when, an' they passed it down to me so we could share it with those who come after us. They say in da ole days, holidays arrived by paddle wheel. The great seasonal event was the coming of the boats.

Now they say there was a feelin' in the air as the young townspeople of Vicksburg gathered before the barrels being rolled into their yards from the waterfront landing. The children would peep into the holes on the side to see what they held. The steamboats brought large grapes, oranges and green bananas by the bunch. The never-before-seen pineapple made its debut by boat and was always placed in the center of the Christmas table, both for its beauty and aroma!

Now, oysters were less exotic, and many families had barrels of them. They would all watch the opening of the shells! My great grandmama said she could hear the "rap, rap, rap" of old Uncle Bob's oyster knife as it pried open the shells and the plump oysters plopped down into the buckets. Back then nothing was wasted. After the shells were opened, they were used to fill the muddy holes of the streets in town.

WOMAN 4 (CONT'D): Vicksburg stood 400 miles or so above New Orleans, and with the winding Mississippi, there came a measure of influence from the Creole city. "Le Grand Boeuf!" was the Christmas beef according to the French townsfolk. Children paraded that poor cow through town, adorned with ribbons and colored garland. Grandmama said he often appeared proud that he had won this role, but not for long as he was soon to reappear on our dinner tables!

While today we get our Christmas beef from the supermarket and not the waterfront, there is still that holiday excitement in the air. The anticipation of what's to come. Christmas is still like that Old River. On December 25th, you never know what you might get!

SONG #11: WHAT THE RIVER MAY HOLD

WOMAN 2 may sing harmony on the chorus with this piece. OTHER LADIES play small percussion instruments (Triangle, washboard, Tambourine, etc.). During second chorus, ALL LADIES move into the audience and play up and down the aisles while singing and wishing audience members "Happy Holidays" and "Merry Christmas".

(Singing)

WE GOT A LOT OF GOOD FOLKS TO SEE
GATHERIN' ROUND LIKE FAMILY
EVERY YEAR WE ALL DO COME
TO SHARE A LAUGH AND HAVE SOME FUN
IT'S ALL GOOD THIS TIME OF YEAR
SHUCK OFF THE BLUES AND LOSE YOUR FEAR
COME ONE COME ALL THE YOUNG AND OLD
THIS TIME OF YEAR, YOU JUST DON'T KNOW

ALL:

WHAT THE RIVER MAY HOLD
IT JUST NEVER GETS OLD
WE'RE ALL WAITIN TO SEE
'BOUT WHAT THE FUTURE MAY BE
'CAUSE YOU NEVER DO KNOW
AN' IT NEVER GETS OLD
OH, THE STORIES DONE TOLD
'BOUT WHAT THE RIVER MAY HOLD

WOMAN 4:

HOLD ON TIGHT AND YOU MAY SEE
A BIG SUPRISE FOR YOU AND ME
DON'T HAVE TO BE WORTH A LOT
CAUSE IT'S ENOUGH, THE LOVE WE GOT

WOMAN 4 (CONT'D):

GOIN' FAST OR GOIN' SLOW
WHAT'S COMIN' ROUND YOU JUST DON'T KNOW
FULL OF LIFE, TREASURES IN TOW
THE MYSTERIES THAT WILL UNFOLD

ALL:

WHAT THE RIVER MAY HOLD
IT JUST NEVER GETS OLD
WE'RE ALL WAITIN' TO SEE
'BOUT WHAT THE FUTURE MAY BE
'CAUSE YOU NEVER DO KNOW
AN' IT NEVER GETS OLD
OH, THE STORIES DONE TOLD
'BOUT WHAT THE RIVER MAY HOLD

ALL WOMEN with hand-held instruments move through the audience dancing and singing to the crowd.

WHAT THE RIVER MAY HOLD
IT JUST NEVER GETS OLD
WE'RE ALL WAITIN TO SEE
'BOUT WHAT THE FUTURE MAY BE
'CAUSE YOU NEVER DO KNOW
AN' IT NEVER GETS OLD
OH, THE STORIES DONE TOLD
'BOUT WHAT THE RIVER MAY HOLD
MYSTERIES WILL UNFOLD
WHAT THE RIVER MAY HOLD
THIS TIME OF YEAR, YA DON'T KNOW
WHAT THE RIVER MAY HOLD
WHAT THE RIVER MAY HOLD
WHAT THE RIVER MAY HOLD

WOMAN 2: "And, lo, the angel of the Lord came upon them, and the glory of the Lord shone round about them: and they were so afraid. And the angel said unto them, Fear not: for, behold, I bring you good tidings of great joy, which shall be to all people. For unto you is born this day in the city of David a Savior, which is Christ the Lord. And this shall be a sign unto you; Ye shall find the babe wrapped in swaddling clothes, lying in a manger. And suddenly there was with the angel a multitude of the heavenly host praising God, and saying, Glory to God in the highest, and on earth peace good will toward men." –Luke 2:9-14

WOMAN 3: I've been a pre-school director for ten years in Louisville, Kentucky. I have had the privilege to see many different children's Christmas musicals, concerts and nativities. All have been beautiful and special to me because they were performed by the children with such excitement and wonder.

WOMAN 3 (CONT'D): The simplicity of the season is found just by looking at a child's face. But one experience stands out to me, one that I will never forget, and one that I personally take a lesson from every year by remembering.

I was visiting another church who was hosting an event depicting that first Christmas night. Excited children waited n line, eager to get inside. I was quickly intrigued with a four-year-old little girl who kept asking, "When can I see Jesus?" We journeyed through "town" seeing basket makers and merchants selling cloth, copper and other items and then we entered the synagogue where the Pharisees studied the scrolls in dim candlelight. Once again you could hear the words of the little girl, "When can we see Jesus?" "Is Jesus here?"

Women baking in a big stone oven offered her a taste of warm sweet bread, but the little girl was having none of that. That was not at all what she had come for. She quickly refused them and pushed towards the crowds that had gathered at the inn. All the characters were reciting well-versed lines, but that didn't stop the little girl from interrupting them. "Where is Jesus?" Without missing a beat they pointed in the other direction. I watched the little girl rush through the crowd to an area that looked like a cave. As she came closer, the noisy crowd there grew quiet. She stopped and drew in an excited breath. She looked down in awe and wonder, but that wasn't enough. She reached out and touched the hand of the real-life baby there. The look on her face said it all. She had seen Jesus. She had done what she came to do. Reflecting back on that night, I am amazed at the persistence of that four-year-old. Her excitement and awe touched the hearts of all who saw her that night.

I often wonder how excited we would get about seeing Jesus. I suppose if we were honest, most of us would admit that we don't have the same zeal that that little girl had. But isn't that what Christmas is all about? When I recall that night, I often pray that even in the business of the season, that we will all have a star struck moment, where we see Him, hear Him and feel his touch. I do hope that we all can find that in our hearts and minds, to see the holiday season through the eyes of a child.

SONG #12: I WANT TO SEE YOU/AWAY IN A MANGER

While WOMAN 3 sings far SL, WOMAN 1 moves to a toy baby crib that lies on SR. Inside the crib is a baby that has been concealed by burlap material. We don't notice the cribs contents until Woman 1 moves to it and kneels down beside it. She pulls the excess burlap out of the crib to cover its sides. The toy is "transformed" into a manger. She pulls out the baby and holds it for just a moment and then places it back into the manger before she stands and sings her verse.

WOMAN 3 (CONT'D):

I WANT TO SEE YOU
I WANT TO FEEL YOU
I HOPE AND PRAY THAT SOMETIMES YOU MAY HEAR ME
FEELING YOUR PRESENCE
LACKING ALL EVIDENCE
FAITH, HOPE AND LOVE IS WHAT MAKES IT ALL CLEAR LORD

WOMAN 1:

AWAY IN A MANGER NO CRIB FOR A BED
THE LITTLE LORD JESUS LAYS DOWN HIS SWEET HEAD
THE STARS IN THE SKY LOOK DOWN WHERE HE LAY
THE LITTLE LORD JESUS ASLEEP ON THE HAY
AWAY IN A MANGER NO CRIB FOR A BED

WOMAN 3:

I WANT TO SEE YOU, I WANT TO FEEL YOU

WOMAN 1:

THE LITTLE LORD JESUS LAYS DOWN HIS SWEET HEAD

WOMAN 3:

I HOPE AND PRAY THAT SOMETIMES YOU MAY HEAR ME

WOMAN 1:

THE STARS IN THE SKY LOOK DOWN WHERE HE LAY

WOMAN 3:

FEELING YOUR PRESENCE, LACKING ALL EVIDENCE

WOMAN 1:

THE LITTLE LORD JESUS ASLEEP ON THE HAY

WOMAN 3:

FAITH, HOPE AND LOVE IS WHAT MAKES IT ALL CLEAR LORD

WOMAN 1:

THE LITTLE LORD JESUS ASLEEP ON THE HAY

WOMAN 3:

FAITH, HOPE AND LOVE IS WHAT MAKES IT ALL CLEAR LORD

"Silent Night" intro plays underneath the dialogue.

WOMAN 2: As far as southern folks go, Christmas is a memory maker, a chance to start anew.

WOMAN 3: Anything can happen at Christmastime and usually does. But no matter where you're from, the one thing that binds us all together is this season's music.

WOMAN 1: Songs with familiar tunes, songs that stand the test of time.

WOMAN 2: Let this season's music help you remember the past and look forward to the future. May you have a most blessed and memorable Christmas.

SONG #13: CHRISTMAS CAROL MEDLEY AND SING-A-LONG

WOMAN 1:
SILENT NIGHT HOLY NIGHT
ALL IS CALM, ALL IS BRIGHT
ROUND YON VIRGIN MOTHER AND CHILD
HOLY INFANT SO TENDER AND MILD
SLEEP IN HEAVENLY PEACE
SLEEP IN HEAVENLY PEACE

WOMAN 2:
OH HOLY NIGHT, THE STARS ARE BIGHTLY SHINING
THIS IS THE NIGHT OF OUR DEAR SAVIOR'S BIRTH
LONG LAY THE WORLD IN SIN AND ERROR PINING
'TIL HE APPEARED AND THE SOUL FELT ITS WORTH
A THRILL OF HOPE, THE WEARLY WORLD REJOICES
FOR YONDER BREAKS THIS NEW AND GLORIOUS MORN
FALL ON YOUR KNEES
OH, HEAR THE ANGEL VOICES
OH NIGHT, DIVINE, OH NIGHT WHEN CHRIST WAS BORN
OH, NIGHT DIVINE, OH NIGHT OH NIGHT DIVINE

WOMAN 3:
JOYFUL, JOYFUL, WE ADORE THEE
GOD OF GLORY, LORD OF LOVE
HEARTS UNFOLD LIKE FLOWERS BEFORE THEE
HAIL THEE AS THE SUN ABOVE
MELT THE CLOUDS OF SIN AND SADNESS
DRIVE THE DARK OF DOUBT AWAY
GIVER OF IMMORTAL GLADNESS
FILL US WITH THE LIGHT
JOYFUL, JOYFUL, WE ADORE THEE
GOD OF GLORY, LORD OF LOVE

WOMAN 4 *(half time)*:
JOY TO THE WORLD, THE LORD IS COME!
LET EARTH RECEIVE HER KING;
LET EVERY HEART PREPARE HIM ROOM,
(Fast tempo)
AND HEAVEN AND NATURE SING,
AND HEAVEN AND NATURE SING,
AND HEAVEN, AND HEAVEN, AND NATURE SING.

ALL: *(Woman 4 improv)*
JOY TO THE EARTH, THE SAVIOR REIGNS!

ALL **(CONT'D):**

LET MEN THEIR SONGS EMPLOY;
WHILE FIELDS AND FLOODS, ROCKS, HILLS AND PLAINS
REPEAT THE SOUNDING JOY,
REPEAT THE SOUNDING JOY,
REPEAT, REPEAT, THE SOUNDING JOY.

JOY TO THE WORLD!

END OF PLAY

Made in the USA
Columbia, SC
11 August 2022

65189493R00026